THE 30-MINUTE SHAKESPEARE
THE COMEDY
OF ERRORS

"Nick Newlin's work as a teaching artist for Folger Education during the past thirteen years has provided students, regardless of their experience with Shakespeare or being on stage, a unique opportunity to tread the boards at the Folger Theatre. Working with students to edit Shakespeare's plays for performance at the annual Folger Shakespeare Festivals has enabled students to gain new insights into the Bard's plays, build their skills of comprehension and critical reading, and just plain have fun working collaboratively with their peers.

Folger Education promotes performance-based teaching of Shakespeare's plays, providing students with an interactive approach to Shakespeare's plays in which they participate in a close reading of the text through intellectual, physical, and vocal engagement. Newlin's *The 30-Minute Shakespeare* series is an invaluable resource for teachers of Shakespeare, and for all who are interested in performing the plays."

ROBERT YOUNG, PH.D.
DIRECTOR OF EDUCATION
FOLGER SHAKESPEARE LIBRARY

Cover design by Sarah Juckniess
Printed in the United States of America

Distributed by Consortium Book Sales & Distribution
www.cbsd.com

NICOLO WHIMSEY PRESS
www.30MinuteShakespeare.com

Art Director: Sarah Juckniess
Managing Editors: Katherine Little, Leah Gordon

THE
COMEDY OF ERRORS

THE 30-MINUTE SHAKESPEARE

Written by **WILLIAM SHAKESPEARE**

Abridged AND Edited
by **NICK NEWLIN**

Nicolo Whimsey
Press

Brandywine, MD

To my brother
Bill Newlin
For turning
words into deeds

**"We came into the world like brother and brother;
And now let's go hand in hand, not one before the other."**

William Shakespeare
The Comedy of Errors
Act V, Scene I

Special thanks to Joanne Flynn, Bill Newlin, Eliza Newlin Carney, William and Louisa Newlin, Michael Tolaydo, Hilary Kacser, Sarah Juckniess, Katherine Little, Eva Zimmerman, Leah Gordon, Frank Harris, Tanya Tolchin, Julie Schaper and all of Consortium, Leo Bowman and the students, faculty, and staff at Banneker Academic High School, and Robert Young Ph.D., and the Folger Shakespeare Library, especially the wonderful Education Department.

✳ TABLE OF CONTENTS

✳ NO EXPERIENCE NECESSARY

I was not a big "actor type" in high school, so if you weren't either, or if the young people you work with are not, then this book is for you. Whether or not you work with "actor types," you can use this book to stage a lively and captivating thirty-minute version of a Shakespeare play. No experience is necessary.

When I was about eleven years old, my parents took me to see Shakespeare's *Two Gentlemen of Verona*, which was being performed as a Broadway musical. I didn't comprehend every word I heard, but I was enthralled with the language, the characters, and the story, and I understood enough of it to follow along. From then on, I associated Shakespeare with *fun*.

Of course Shakespeare is fun. The Elizabethan audiences knew it, which is one reason he was so popular. It didn't matter that some of the language eluded them. The characters were passionate and vibrant, and their conflicts were compelling. Young people study Shakespeare in high school, but more often than not they read his work like a text book and then get quizzed on academic elements of the play, such as plot, theme, and vocabulary. These are all very interesting, but not nearly as interesting as standing up and performing a scene! It is through performance that the play comes alive and all its "academic" elements are revealed. There is nothing more satisfying to a student or teacher than the feeling of "owning" a Shakespeare play, and that can only come from performing it.

But Shakespeare's plays are often two or more hours long, making the performance of an entire play almost out of the question. One can perform a single scene, which is certainly a good start, but what about the story? What about the changes a character goes through as the play progresses? When school groups perform one scene unedited, or when they lump several plays together, the audience can get lost. This is why I have always preferred to tell the story of the play.

The 30-Minute Shakespeare gives students and teachers a chance to get up on their feet and act out a Shakespeare play in half an hour, using his language. The emphasis is on key scenes, with narrative bridges between scenes to keep the audience caught up on the action. The stage directions are built into this script so that young actors do not have to stand in one place; they can move and tell the story with their actions as well as their words. And it can all be done in a classroom during class time!

That is where this book was born: not in a research library, a graduate school lecture, a professional stage, or even an after-school drama club. All of the play cuttings in *The 30-Minute Shakespeare* were first rehearsed in a D.C. public high school English class, and performed successfully at the Folger Shakespeare Library's annual Secondary School Shakespeare Festival. The players were not necessarily "actor types." For many of them, this was their first performance in a play.

Something almost miraculous happens when students perform Shakespeare. They "get" it. By occupying the characters and speaking the words out loud, students gain a level of understanding and appreciation that is unachievable by simply reading the text. That is the magic of a performance-based method of learning Shakespeare, and this book makes the formerly daunting task of staging a Shakespeare play possible for anybody.

With *The 30-Minute Shakespeare* book series I hope to help teachers and students produce a Shakespeare play in a short amount of time, thus jump-starting the process of discovering the beauty, magic, and fun of the Bard. Plot, theme, and language reveal themselves through the performance of these half-hour play cuttings, and everybody involved receives the priceless gift of "owning" a piece of Shakespeare. The result is an experience that is fun and engaging, and one that we can all carry with us as we play out our own lives on the stages of the world.

NICK NEWLIN
Brandywine, MD
March 2010

CHARACTERS IN THE PLAY

The following is a list of characters that appear in this cutting of
The Comedy of Errors.

Twenty-six actors performed in the original production. This
number can be increased to about thirty or decreased to about
twelve by having actors share or double roles.

For the full breakdown of characters, see Sample Program.

DUKE SOLINUS: Duke of Ephesus

EGEON: A merchant of Syracuse

YOUNG EGEON

JAILER

FIRST MERCHANT

ANTIPHOLUS OF EPHESUS ⟩ Twin brothers, and sons
ANTIPHOLUS OF SYRACUSE to Egeon and Emilia

DROMIO OF EPHESUS ⟩ Twin brothers, and bondsmen
DROMIO OF SYRACUSE to the two Antipholuses

ADRIANA: Wife to Antipholus of Ephesus

LUCIANA: Her sister

ANGELO: A goldsmith

SECOND MERCHANT

EMILIA: Wife to Egeon, an abbess at Ephesus

SERVANT

NARRATORS

✳ SCENE 1. (ACT I, SCENE I)

A hall in Duke Solinus's palace.

Stagehands set throne at an angle stage right, downstage of pillars, then set chair stage left, downstage of pillars and slightly facing throne.

Enter NARRATOR *from stage rear, coming downstage center.*

NARRATOR

> Our play begins with Egeon sentenced to death for trespassing in Ephesus. He explains to the Duke how he became separated from his wife and two sets of twins.

Exit NARRATOR *stage left.*

Enter DUKE SOLINUS, EGEON, *and* JAILER *from stage right.* DUKE SOLINUS *sits in throne.* JAILER *enters with* EGEON *in cuffs and stands center stage, facing* EGEON, *who is slightly downstage.*

EGEON

> Proceed, Solinus, to procure my fall
> And by the doom of death end woes and all.

DUKE SOLINUS

> Merchant of Syracuse, plead no more;
> I am not partial to infringe our laws:
> Again: if any Syracusian born
> Come to the bay of Ephesus, he dies,

Unless a thousand marks be levied,
Therefore by law thou art condemned to die.

EGEON

Yet this my comfort: when your words are done,
My woes end likewise with the evening sun.

DUKE SOLINUS

Well, Syracusian, say in brief the cause
Why thou departed'st from thy native home
And for what cause thou camest to Ephesus.

EGEON

In Syracusa was I born, and wed
Unto a woman, happy but for me,
A joyful mother of two goodly sons;
And, which was strange, the one so like the other,
As could not be distinguish'd but by names.

Enter **EGEON'S WIFE** *and* **SONS** *from stage rear. The* **SONS** *stand on either side of their mother, upstage right.*

That very hour, and in the self-same inn,
A meaner woman was delivered
Of such a burden, male twins, both alike:

Enter **TWINS** *from stage rear, moving upstage left.*

Those,—for their parents were exceeding poor,—
I bought and brought up to attend my sons.

Enter **YOUNG EGEON** *from stage rear.* **ALL** *move toward center, remaining upstage.*

A league from Epidamnum had we sail'd,
Before the always wind-obeying deep

Gave doubtful warrant of immediate death;
The sailors sought for safety by our boat,
And left the ship, then sinking-ripe, to us:
My wife, more careful for the latter-born,
Had fasten'd him unto a small spare mast,
To him one of the other twins was bound,

EGEON'S WIFE *affixes one of her sons and one of the adopted twins to the right side of a long pole.*

Whilst I had been like heedful of the other:

YOUNG EGEON *affixes the other of his sons and the other adopted twin to the left side of the pole.*

The children thus disposed, my wife and I,
Fasten'd ourselves at either end the mast;

EGEON'S WIFE *affixes herself to right side of pole, as* YOUNG EGEON *affixes himself to the left.*

We were encounterd by a mighty rock;
Our helpful ship was splitted in the midst.
Her part, poor soul
Was carried with more speed before the wind.

The pole splits in half and the two groups exit the stage on their respective sides.

Thus have you heard me sever'd from my bliss;
And happy were I in my timely death,
Could all my travels warrant me they live.

DUKE SOLINUS *(stands)*
Hapless Egeon, whom the fates have mark'd
To bear the extremity of dire mishap!
But, though thou art adjudged to the death

      Yet I will favor thee in what I can. *(motions for*
               JAILER *to unshackle* EGEON*)*
      Therefore, merchant, I'll limit thee this day;
      Beg thou, or borrow, to make up the sum,
      And live; if no, then thou art doom'd to die.
      Jailer, take him to thy custody.

JAILER

      I will, my lord.

EGEON

      Hopeless and helpless doth Egeon wend,
      But to procrastinate his lifeless end.

Exit DUKE SOLINUS *stage left.* EGEON *and* JAILER *follow.*

STAGEHANDS *remove throne and chair, set bench downstage center.*

✳ SCENE 2. (ACT I, SCENE II)

The Mart.

Enter **NARRATOR** *from stage rear, coming downstage center.*

NARRATOR

> Antipholus of Syracuse and his servant, Dromio
> of Syracuse, have traveled to Ephesus in search
> of their long lost twin brothers and their mother.
> Antipholus gives money to Dromio of Syracuse.
> Dromio's twin, Dromio of Ephesus, returns, and
> the confusion begins!

Exit **NARRATOR** *stage left.*

Enter **ANTIPHOLUS OF SYRACUSE, DROMIO OF SYRACUSE,** *and*
FIRST MERCHANT *from stage right. All stand in front of bench,*
with **ANTIPHOLUS** *center,* **DROMIO** *to his right, and* **FIRST MERCHANT**
to his left.

FIRST MERCHANT

> Therefore give out you are of Epidamnum;
> This very day a Syracusian merchant
> Dies ere the weary sun set in the west.
> There is your money that I had to keep.
> > *(hands bag of money to* **DROMIO***)*

DROMIO OF SYRACUSE

> Many a man would take you at your word,
> And go indeed, having so good a mean.

ANTIPHOLUS OF SYRACUSE (*to* DROMIO)
>Go bear it to the Centaur, where we host,
>And stay there, Dromio, till I come to thee.
>Within this hour it will be dinner-time:
>Get thee away.

Exit DROMIO OF SYRACUSE *stage right.*

ANTIPHOLUS OF SYRACUSE (*to* FIRST MERCHANT)
>A trusty villain, sir, that very oft,
>When I am dull with care and melancholy,
>Lightens my humor with his merry jests.

FIRST MERCHANT
>Sir, I commend you to your own content.

Exit FIRST MERCHANT *stage left.*

ANTIPHOLUS OF SYRACUSE (*walks downstage center*)
>He that commends me to mine own content
>Commends me to the thing I cannot get.
>I to the world am like a drop of water
>That in the ocean seeks another drop,
>Who, falling there to find his fellow forth,
>Unseen, inquisitive, confounds himself:
>So I, to find a mother and a brother,
>In quest of them, unhappy, lose myself.

Enter DROMIO OF EPHESUS *from stage right.*

>Here comes the almanac of my true date.
>What now? How chance thou art return'd so soon?

DROMIO OF EPHESUS
>Return'd so soon! Rather approach'd too late:
>My mistress made it one upon my cheek:

She is so hot because the meat is cold;
The meat is cold because you come not home.

ANTIPHOLUS OF SYRACUSE
Stop in your wind, sir: tell me this, I pray:
Where have you left the money that I gave you?

DROMIO OF EPHESUS
To me, sir? Why, you gave no gold to me.

ANTIPHOLUS OF SYRACUSE
Come on, sir knave, have done your foolishness,
And tell me how thou hast disposed thy charge.

DROMIO OF EPHESUS
My charge was but to fetch you from the mart
Home to your house, the Phoenix, sir, to dinner:
My mistress and her sister stays for you.
(gestures toward stage right)

ANTIPHOLUS OF SYRACUSE
What, wilt thou flout me thus unto my face,
Being forbid? There, take you that, sir knave.
(beats DROMIO *with his hat)*

DROMIO OF EPHESUS *(covers face with hands and sinks to knees)*
What mean you, sir? For God's sake, hold your
hands!

ANTIPHOLUS *keeps hitting him;* DROMIO *is now lying on his back on the floor.*

Nay, and you will not, sir, I'll take my heels.

Exit DROMIO OF EPHESUS *stage right.* ANTIPHOLUS *throws his hat after him.*

ANTIPHOLUS OF SYRACUSE

    Upon my life, by some device or other
    The villain is o'er-raught of all my money.
    I'll to the Centaur, to go seek this slave:
    I greatly fear my money is not safe.

Exit ANTIPHOLUS *stage right.*

STAGEHANDS *move bench to center stage, setting it at an angle facing stage right.*

✳ SCENE 3. (ACT II, SCENE II)

Outside of Antipholus of Ephesus's house.

Enter NARRATOR *from stage rear, coming downstage center.*

NARRATOR
> Now Dromio of Syracuse, our first Dromio, comes back and has no idea why Antipholus of Syracuse thinks he was just there. They wind up at the house of Adriana, who thinks Antipholus of Syracuse is actually Antipholus of Ephesus, her husband and his twin—who we haven't met yet. Confused? Good! So are they!

Exit NARRATOR *stage left.*

Enter ANTIPHOLUS OF SYRACUSE *from stage rear; he stands in front of bench.*

ANTIPHOLUS OF SYRACUSE
> The gold I gave to Dromio is laid up
> Safe at the Centaur; I could not speak with Dromio
> > since at first
> I sent him from the mart. See, here he comes.

Enter DROMIO OF SYRACUSE *from stage right.*

ANTIPHOLUS OF SYRACUSE
> How now sir! Is your merry humor alter'd?
> Jest with me again. You received no gold?
> Your mistress sent to have me home to dinner?

DROMIO OF SYRACUSE
> I did not see you since you sent me hence,
> with the gold you gave me.

ANTIPHOLUS OF SYRACUSE
> Think'st thou I jest? Hold, take thou that, and that.
> *(beats* DROMIO *with his hat)*

ANTIPHOLUS *chases* DROMIO *around the bench.*

DROMIO OF SYRACUSE
> But, I pray, sir why am I beaten?

ANTIPHOLUS OF SYRACUSE
> For flouting me.

ANTIPHOLUS *chases* DROMIO *again, hitting him with his hat.*
The chase ends with both sitting on the bench.

DROMIO OF SYRACUSE
> Well, sir, I thank you.

ANTIPHOLUS OF SYRACUSE
> Thank me, sir, for what?

DROMIO OF SYRACUSE
> Marry, sir, for this something that you gave me
> for nothing.

Enter ADRIANA *and* LUCIANA *from stage right. As* ADRIANA
approaches ANTIPHOLUS, DROMIO *gets up and stands behind bench.*

ADRIANA
> Ay, ay, Antipholus, look strange and frown:
> Some other mistress hath thy sweet aspects;
> I am not Adriana nor thy wife.

ADRIANA *grabs* ANTIPHOLUS'S *arm; he moves farther down the*
bench, and ADRIANA *falls onto it.*

> Ah, do not tear away thyself from me!
> For know, my love, as easy mayest thou fall
> A drop of water in the breaking gulf,
> And take unmingled that same drop again,
> Without addition or diminishing,
> As take from me thyself and not me too. *(stands)*
> How dearly would it touch me to the quick,
> Shouldst thou but hear I were licentious
> Wouldst thou not spit at me and spurn at me
> And hurl the name of husband in my face
> And from my false hand cut the wedding-ring
> I know thou canst; and therefore see thou do it.

ADRIANA *walks downstage center and addresses the audience.*

> I am possess'd with an adulterate blot;
> My blood is mingled with the crime of lust:
> > *(sits again on bench, but not directly next*
> > *to* ANTIPHOLUS*)*
> For if we two be one and thou play false,
> I do digest the poison of thy flesh,
> Being strumpeted by thy contagion.

ADRIANA *turns her back to* ANTIPHOLUS *and pauses. She looks*
over her shoulder at him and sees he is bewildered. She softens,
moves back toward him on the bench, and holds his hand. He
allows her to do it but remains confused.

> Keep then fair league and truce with thy true bed;
> I live distain'd, thou undishonored.

ANTIPHOLUS OF SYRACUSE *(lets go of her hand and stands)*
> Plead you to me, fair dame? I know you not.

LUCIANA
>Fie, brother! How the world is changed with you!
>When were you wont to use my sister thus?
>She sent for you by Dromio home to dinner.

ANTIPHOLUS OF SYRACUSE
>By Dromio?

DROMIO OF SYRACUSE
>By me?

ADRIANA
>By thee.

ANTIPHOLUS OF SYRACUSE *(to* DROMIO*)*
>How can she thus then call us by our names,
>Unless it be by inspiration?

ADRIANA *(stands, faces* ANTIPHOLUS*)*
>How ill agrees it with your gravity
>To counterfeit thus grossly with your slave,
>Abetting him to thwart me in my mood!
>>*(tries a gentler approach, holding his arm)*
>Come, I will fasten on this sleeve of thine:
>Thou art an elm, my husband, I a vine.

ANTIPHOLUS OF SYRACUSE *(walks downstage center,*
>*addressing audience)*
>To me she speaks; she moves me for her theme:
>What, was I married to her in my dream?

DROMIO OF SYRACUSE *(walks downstage center, addressing*
>*audience)*
>This is the fairy land: O spite of spites!
>We talk with goblins, owls and sprites.

LUCIANA

> Why pratest thou to thyself and answer'st not?
> Dromio, thou drone, thou snail, thou slug, thou sot!

DROMIO OF SYRACUSE (*to* ANTIPHOLUS)

> I am transformed, master; I am an ape.

LUCIANA

> If thou art changed to aught, 'tis to an ass.

DROMIO OF SYRACUSE

> 'Tis true; she rides me and I long for grass.
> 'Tis so, I am an ass; else it could never be
> But I should know her as well as she knows me.

ANTIPHOLUS OF SYRACUSE

> Am I in earth, in heaven, or in hell?
> Sleeping or waking? Mad or well-advised?
> Known unto these, and to myself disguised!
> I'll say as they say and persever so,
> And in this mist at all adventures go.

DROMIO OF SYRACUSE

> Master, shall I be porter at the gate?

ADRIANA *takes* DROMIO *by the ear and leads him stage right.*

ADRIANA

> Ay; and let none enter, lest I break your pate.

LUCIANA

> Come, come, Antipholus, we dine too late.

Exit ADRIANA, LUCIANA, *and* ANTIPHOLUS *stage rear.* DROMIO *looks to stage right entrance, looks to audience, shrugs, and exits stage right.*

* SCENE 4. (ACT III, SCENE II)

Outside of Antipholus of Ephesus's house.

Enter NARRATOR *from stage rear, coming downstage center.*

NARRATOR
> Meanwhile, Antipholus of Syracuse falls for Luciana,
> who is the sister of Antipholus of Ephesus's wife,
> Adriana, who thinks this Antipholus is her husband,
> but he isn't. Are you following this? Don't worry
> about it. Neither are they.

Exit NARRATOR *stage left.*

Enter LUCIANA *and* ANTIPHOLUS OF SYRACUSE *from stage left.*
They stand in front of bench.

LUCIANA
> And may it be that you have quite forgot
> A husband's office? Shall, Antipholus,
> Even in the spring of love, thy love-springs rot?
> Muffle your false love with some show of blindness:
> Let not my sister read it in your eye;
> Comfort my sister, cheer her, call her wife:
> 'Tis holy sport to be a little vain,
> When the sweet breath of flattery conquers strife.
> *(sits on downstage side of bench)*

ANTIPHOLUS OF SYRACUSE
> Your weeping sister is no wife of mine,
> Nor to her bed no homage do I owe

Far more, far more to you do I decline.
(sits next to LUCIANA *on bench)*

LUCIANA *hesitates, enjoying the closeness, then turns to look at* ANTIPHOLUS. *She stands and backs away a step.*

LUCIANA

What, are you mad, that you do reason so?

ANTIPHOLUS OF SYRACUSE

Not mad, but mated; how, I do not know.
(stands; steps toward LUCIANA*)*

LUCIANA

Why call you me love? Call my sister so. *(steps back)*

ANTIPHOLUS OF SYRACUSE

Call thyself sister, sweet, for I am thee.
Thee will I love and with thee lead my life:
Thou hast no husband yet nor I no wife.
Give me thy hand.

ANTIPHOLUS *takes a final step toward* LUCIANA *and takes her hand. He pauses.*

LUCIANA

O, soft, sir! Hold you still: *(lets go of his hand;*
turns away)
I'll fetch my sister, to get her good will.

Exit LUCIANA *stage left.*

Enter DROMIO OF SYRACUSE *from stage left, running and out of breath.*

ANTIPHOLUS OF SYRACUSE

Why, how now, Dromio! Where runn'st thou so fast?

DROMIO OF SYRACUSE
> I am an ass, I am a woman's man and besides myself.
> *(steps to the side; looks behind him)*

ANTIPHOLUS OF SYRACUSE *(interested and amused)*
> What woman's man? What is she?

DROMIO OF SYRACUSE
> She's the kitchen wench and all grease; *(looks stage
> left)* She is spherical, like a globe; I could find out
> countries in her. This drudge, or diviner, laid claim
> to me, call'd me Dromio; swore I was assured to her;
> told me what privy marks I had about me, as the
> mole in my neck, the great wart on my left arm, that
> I amazed ran from her as a witch.

ANTIPHOLUS OF SYRACUSE *(to* **DROMIO**, *in a stage whisper)*
> Go hie thee presently, post to the road:
> I will not harbor in this town to-night:
> If every one knows us and we know none,
> 'Tis time, I think, to trudge, pack and be gone.

DROMIO OF SYRACUSE
> As from a bear a man would run for life,
> So fly I from her that would be my wife.

Exit **DROMIO OF SYRACUSE** *stage right.*

ANTIPHOLUS OF SYRACUSE
> There's none but witches do inhabit here;
> But, lest myself be guilty to self-wrong,
> I'll stop mine ears against the mermaid's song.

Enter **ANGELO** *from stage right, holding a chain.*

ANGELO
>Master Antipholus,—

ANTIPHOLUS OF SYRACUSE *(startled)*
>Ay, that's my name.

ANGELO *(pause)*
>I know it well, sir, lo, here is the chain.

ANTIPHOLUS OF SYRACUSE *(pause)*
>What is your will that I shall do with this?

ANGELO *(pause)*
>What please yourself, sir: I have made it for you.

ANTIPHOLUS OF SYRACUSE
>Made it for me, sir! I bespoke it not.

ANGELO
>Not once, nor twice, but twenty times you have.
>Go home with it and please your wife withal;
>And soon at supper-time I'll visit you
>And then receive my money for the chain.

ANTIPHOLUS OF SYRACUSE
>I pray you, sir, receive the money now,
>For fear you ne'er see chain nor money more.

ANGELO *(pause)*
>You are a merry man, sir: fare you well.

Exit ANGELO *stage right.*

ANTIPHOLUS OF SYRACUSE
>What I should think of this, I cannot tell:

> I'll to the mart, and there for Dromio stay
> If any ship put out, then straight away.

Exit ANTIPHOLUS OF SYRACUSE *stage right.*

STAGEHANDS *remove bench.*

✳ SCENE 5. (ACT V, SCENE I)

A street before a Priory.

Enter NARRATOR *from stage rear, coming downstage center.*

NARRATOR
> Meanwhile, Angelo the goldsmith has met
> Antipholus of Syracuse's twin, Antipholus of Ephesus,
> who has denied ever receiving a chain. Antipholus
> of Ephesus finally shows up, furious that he has been
> locked out of his house and abused. There is more
> confusion! We are praying for a happy ending!

Exit NARRATOR *stage left.*

Enter SECOND MERCHANT *and* ANGELO *from stage right.*

ANGELO
> I am sorry, sir, that I have hinder'd you;
> But, I protest, he had the chain of me,
> Though most dishonestly he doth deny it.

SECOND MERCHANT
> Speak softly; yonder, as I think, he walks.

ANGELO *and* SECOND MERCHANT *hide behind stage right pillar.*

Enter ANTIPHOLUS OF SYRACUSE *and* DROMIO OF SYRACUSE *from stage right.*

ANGELO *(stage whispers)*
> 'Tis so; and that self chain about his neck
> Which he forswore most monstrously to have.
> Good sir, draw near to me, I'll speak to him.
> > *(raises voice)*
> Signior Antipholus,
> This chain you had of me; can you deny it?

ANTIPHOLUS OF SYRACUSE
> I think I had; I never did deny it.

SECOND MERCHANT
> Yes, that you did, sir, and forswore it too.

ANTIPHOLUS OF SYRACUSE
> Thou art a villain to impeach me thus:
> I'll prove mine honor and mine honesty
> Against thee presently, if thou darest stand.

SECOND MERCHANT
> I dare, and do defy thee for a villain.

They draw swords and prepare to fight.

Enter ADRIANA *and* LUCIANA *from stage right.*

ADRIANA
> Hold, hurt him not, for God's sake! He is mad.
> Some get within him, take his sword away:
> Bind Dromio too, and bear them to my house.

DROMIO OF SYRACUSE
> Run, master, run; for God's sake, take a house!
> This is some priory. In, or we are spoil'd!

Exit ANTIPHOLUS OF SYRACUSE *and* DROMIO OF SYRACUSE *stage rear.*

Enter EMILIA, *the Abbess, from stage rear.*

EMILIA

Be quiet, people. Wherefore throng you hither?

ADRIANA

To fetch my poor distracted husband hence.
Let us come in, that we may bind him fast.

ADRIANA *tries to exit stage rear into the Priory, but* EMILIA *blocks her way, no matter which path she tries.*

EMILIA

No, not a creature enters in my house.
He took this place for sanctuary.
Therefore depart and leave him here with me.

ADRIANA

I will not hence and leave my husband here:
And ill it doth beseem your holiness
To separate the husband and the wife.

EMILIA

Be quiet and depart: thou shalt not have him.

Exit EMILIA *stage rear.*

SOUND OPERATOR *plays* Sound Cue #1 ("Fanfare").

Enter DUKE SOLINUS *and* EGEON *from stage right.* EGEON *stands in front of stage left pillar, his wrists bound by rope.*

LUCIANA

Complain unto the duke of this indignity.

DUKE SOLINUS

Yet once again proclaim it publicly,
If any friend will pay the sum for him,
He shall not die; so much we tender him.

ADRIANA *(bows to* DUKE SOLINUS*)*

Justice, most sacred duke, against the abbess!

DUKE SOLINUS

She is a virtuous and a reverend lady:
It cannot be that she hath done thee wrong.

ADRIANA

May it please your grace, Antipholus, my husband,
This ill day, a most outrageous fit of madness took
    him;
That desperately he hurried through the street,
With him his bondman, all as mad as he—
Then they fled into this abbey, whither we pursued
    them:
And here the abbess shuts the gates on us.

DUKE SOLINUS

Go, some of you, knock at the abbey-gate
And bid the lady abbess come to me.
I will determine this before I stir.

Enter SERVANT *from stage right.*

SERVANT

O mistress, mistress, shift and save yourself!
My master and his man are both broke loose,

ADRIANA

Peace, fool! Thy master and his man are here,
And that is false thou dost report to us.

SERVANT
>Mistress, upon my life, I tell you true.

Enter ANTIPHOLUS OF EPHESUS *and* DROMIO OF EPHESUS *from stage right.*

ADRIANA
>Ay me, it is my husband! Witness you,
>That he is borne about invisible:
>Even now we housed him in the abbey here;
>And now he's there, past thought of human reason.

ANTIPHOLUS OF EPHESUS *(bows)*
>Justice, most gracious duke, O, grant me justice!

EGEON *(steps forward, addressing audience)*
>Unless the fear of death doth make me dote,
>I see my son Antipholus and Dromio.

ANTIPHOLUS OF EPHESUS
>Justice, sweet princess, against that woman there!
>She whom thou gavest to me to be my wife,
>Beyond imagination is the wrong
>That she this day hath shameless thrown on me.

DUKE SOLINUS *(stands, with* ANTIPHOLUS *to his right and*
>   LUCIANA *and* LUCIANA *to his left)*
>Discover how, and thou shalt find me just.

ANTIPHOLUS OF EPHESUS
>This day, great duke, she shut the doors upon me,
>While she with harlots feasted in my house.
>   *(points stage left)*

DUKE SOLINUS
>A grievous fault! Say, woman, didst thou so?

ADRIANA

No, my good lord: myself, he and my sister
To-day did dine together.

DUKE SOLINUS

Saw'st thou him enter at the abbey here?

ADRIANA

As sure, my liege, as I do see your grace.

DUKE SOLINUS

Why, this is strange. Go call the abbess hither.
I think you are all mated or stark mad.

Exit LUCIANA *stage rear.*

EGEON

Most mighty duke, vouchsafe me speak a word:
            (bows)
Haply I see a friend will save my life
And pay the sum that may deliver me.

DUKE SOLINUS

Speak freely, Syracusian, what thou wilt.

EGEON *(approaches* ANTIPHOLUS*)*

Is not your name, sir, call'd Antipholus?
And is not that your bondman, Dromio?
Why look you strange on me? You know me well.

ANTIPHOLUS OF EPHESUS

I never saw you in my life till now.

EGEON

O, grief hath changed me since you saw me last,
And careful hours with time's deformed hand

Have written strange defeatures in my face:
But tell me yet, dost thou not know my voice?

ANTIPHOLUS OF EPHESUS
Neither.

EGEON
Dromio, nor thou?

DROMIO OF EPHESUS
No, trust me, sir, nor I.

EGEON (*steps downstage center, addressing audience*)
Not know my voice! O time's extremity,
Hast thou so crack'd and splitted my poor tongue
In seven short years, that here my only son
Knows not my feeble key of untuned cares?
(*turns toward* **ANTIPHOLUS**)
Tell me thou art my son Antipholus.

ANTIPHOLUS OF EPHESUS
I never saw my father in my life.

EGEON, *devastated, stumbles back toward stage left and almost collapses from dismay.*

Enter **EMILIA** *from stage rear with* **ANTIPHOLUS OF SYRACUSE** *and* **DROMIO OF SYRACUSE.**

EMILIA
Most mighty duke, behold a man much wrong'd.

ALL *gather to look at the men.*

ADRIANA
I see two husbands, or mine eyes deceive me.

DUKE SOLINUS

> One of these men is Genius to the other;
> And so of these. Which is the natural man,
> And which the spirit? Who deciphers them?

DROMIO OF SYRACUSE

> I, sir, am Dromio; command him away.

DROMIO OF EPHESUS

> I, sir, am Dromio; pray, let me stay.

ANTIPHOLUS OF SYRACUSE

> Egeon art thou not? Or else his ghost?

DROMIO OF SYRACUSE

> O, my old master! Who hath bound him here?
> *(indignant)*

EMILIA

> Whoever bound him, I will loose his bonds
> *(she unties EGEON'S wrists)*
> And gain a husband by his liberty.
> Speak, old Egeon, if thou be'st the man
> That hadst a wife once call'd Emilia
> That bore thee at a burden two fair sons:
> O, if thou be'st the same Egeon, speak,
> And speak unto the same Emilia!

EGEON

> If I dream not, thou art Emilia:
> If thou art she, tell me where is that son
> That floated with thee on the fatal raft?

EMILIA

> What then became of them I cannot tell *(pauses)*
> I to this fortune that you see me in.

DUKE SOLINUS

> Why, here begins his morning story right;
> These two Antipholuses, these two so like,
> And these two Dromios, one in semblance,—
> These are the parents to these children,
> Which accidentally are met together.

ADRIANA

> Which of you two did dine with me to-day?

ANTIPHOLUS OF SYRACUSE

> I, gentle mistress.

ADRIANA

> And are not you my husband?

ANTIPHOLUS OF EPHESUS

> No; I say nay to that.

ANTIPHOLUS OF SYRACUSE

> And so do I; yet did she call me so:
> And this fair gentlewoman, her sister here,
> Did call me brother. *(to* LUCIANA*)*
> What I told you then,
> I hope I shall have leisure to make good;
> If this be not a dream I see and hear.

ANGELO

> That is the chain, sir, which you had of me.

ANTIPHOLUS OF SYRACUSE

> I think it be, sir; I deny it not.

ANTIPHOLUS OF EPHESUS

> And you, sir, for this chain arrested me.

ANGELO

I think I did, sir; I deny it not.

ANTIPHOLUS OF EPHESUS

These ducats pawn I for my father here.

ANTIPHOLUS OF EPHESEUS *offers a bag of money to* DUKE SOLINUS, *but the* DUKE *refuses it.*

DUKE SOLINUS

It shall not need; thy father hath his life.

EMILIA

Thirty-three years have I but gone in travail
Of you, my sons; and till this present hour
My heavy burden ne'er delivered.

The rest of the cast and crew start to enter from stage right, left, and rear, as if the news has spread through the town and they are coming to witness the twins and the reunion of the long lost family.

The duke, my husband and my children both,
And you the calendars of their nativity,
Go to a gossips' feast and go with me;
After so long grief, such nativity!

DUKE SOLINUS

With all my heart, I'll gossip at this feast.

THE TWO ANTIPHOLUSES AND THE TWO DROMIOS

We came into the world like brother and brother;
And now let's go hand in hand, not one before
another.

Entire cast repeats the line at top volume, holding hands and facing the audience.

ALL

> We came into the world like brother and brother;
> And now let's go hand in hand, not one before the
> other!

ALL *raise hands together with an increasingly loud cheer and take a bow. Exeunt.*

✳ PERFORMING SHAKESPEARE

HOW *THE 30-MINUTE SHAKESPEARE* WAS BORN

In 1981 I performed a "Shakespeare Juggling" piece called "To Juggle or Not To Juggle" at the first Folger Library Secondary School Shakespeare Festival. The audience consisted of about 200 Washington, D.C. area high school students who had just performed thirty-minute versions of Shakespeare plays for each other and were jubilant over the experience. I was dressed in a jester's outfit, and my job was to entertain them. I juggled and jested and played with Shakespeare's words, notably Hamlet's "To be or not to be" soliloquy, to very enthusiastic response. I was struck by how much my "Shakespeare Juggling" resonated with a group who had just performed Shakespeare themselves. "Getting" Shakespeare is a heady feeling, especially for adolescents, and I am continually delighted at how much joy and satisfaction young people derive from performing Shakespeare. Simply reading and studying this great playwright does not even come close to inspiring the kind of enthusiasm that comes from performance.

Surprisingly, many of these students were not "actor types." A good percentage of the students performing Shakespeare that day were part of an English class which had rehearsed the plays during class time. Fifteen years later, when I first started directing plays in D.C. public schools as a Teaching Artist with the Folger Shakespeare Library, I entered a ninth grade English class as a guest and spent two or three days a week for two or three months preparing students for the Folger's annual Secondary School Shakespeare Festival. I have conducted this annual residency with the Folger ever since. Every year for seven action-packed days, eight groups of students between grades seven and twelve tread the boards onstage at the Folger's Elizabethan Theatre, a grand recreation of a sixteenth-century venue with a three-tiered gallery, carved oak columns, and a sky-painted canopy.

As noted on the Folger website (www.folger.edu), "The festival is a celebration of the Bard, not a competition. Festival commentators—drawn from the professional theater and Shakespeare education communities—recognize exceptional performances, student directors, and good spirit amongst the students with selected awards at the end of each day. They are also available to share feedback with the students."

My annual Folger Teaching Artist engagement, directing a Shakespeare play in a public high school English class, is the most challenging and the most rewarding thing I do all year. I hope this book can bring you the same rewards.

GETTING STARTED

GAMES

How can you get an English class (or any other group of young people, or even adults) to start the seemingly daunting task of performing a Shakespeare play? You have already successfully completed the critical first step, which is buying this book. You hold in your hand a performance-ready, thirty-minute cutting of a Shakespeare play, with stage directions to get the actors moving about the stage purposefully. But it's a good idea to warm the group up with some theater games.

One good initial exercise is called "Positive/Negative Salutations." Students stand in two lines facing each other (four or five students in each line) and, reading from index cards, greet each other, first with a "Positive" salutation in Shakespeare's language (using actual phrases from the plays), followed by a "negative" greeting.

Additionally, short vocal exercises are an essential part of the preparation process. The following is a very simple and effective vocal warm-up: Beginning with the number two, have the whole group count to twenty using increments of two (i.e., "Two, four, six . . ."). Increase the volume slightly with each number, reaching top volume with "twenty," and then decrease the volume while counting back down, so that the students are practically whispering when they arrive again at "two." This exercise teaches dynamics and allows them to get loud as a group without any individual pressure. Frequently during a rehearsal period, if a student is mumbling inaudibly, I will refer back to this exercise as a reminder that we can and often do belt it out!

"Stomping Words" is a game that is very helpful at getting a handle on Shakespeare's rhythm. Choose a passage in iambic pentameter and have the group members walk around the room in a circle, stomping their feet on the second beat of each line:

Two **house**-holds, **both** a-**like** in **dig**-nity
In **fair** Ve-**ro**na **Where** we **lay** our **scene**

Do the same thing with a prose passage, and have the students discuss their experience with it, including points at which there is an extra beat, etc., and what, if anything, it might signify.

I end every vocal warm-up with a group reading of one of the speeches from the play, emphasizing diction and projection, bouncing off consonants, and encouraging the group members to listen to each other so that they can speak the lines together in unison. For variety I will throw in some classic "tongue twisters" too, such as, "The sixth sheik's sixth sheep is sick."

The Folger Shakespeare Library's website (http://www.folger.edu) and their book series *Shakespeare Set Free,* edited by Peggy O'Brien, are two great resources for getting started with a performance-based teaching of Shakespeare in the classroom. The Folger website has numerous helpful resources and activities, many submitted by teachers, for helping a class actively participate in the process of getting to know a Shakespeare play. For more simple theater games, Viola Spolin's *Theatre Games for the Classroom* is very helpful, as is one I use frequently, *Theatre Games for Young Performers.*

HATS AND PROPS

Introducing a few hats and props early in the process is a good way to get the action going. Hats, in particular, provide a nice avenue for giving young actors a non-verbal way of getting into character. In the opening weeks, when students are still holding onto their scripts, a hat can give an actor a way to "feel" like a character. Young actors are natural masters at injecting their own personality into what they wear, and even small choices made with how a hat is worn (jauntily, shadily, cockily, mysteriously) provide a starting point for discussion of specific characters, their traits, and their relationships with other characters. All such discussions always lead back to one thing: the text. "Mining the text" is consistently the best strategy for uncovering the mystery of Shakespeare's language. That is where all the answers lie: in the words themselves.

WHAT DO THE WORDS MEAN?

It is essential that young actors know what they are saying when they recite Shakespeare. If not, they might as well be scat singing, riffing on sounds and rhythm but not conveying a specific meaning. The real question is: What do the words mean? The answer is multifaceted, and can be found in more than one place. The New Folger Library paperback editions of the plays themselves (edited by Barbara Mowat and Paul Werstine, Washington Square Press) are a great resource for understanding Shakespeare's words and passages and "translating" them into modern English. These editions also contain chapters on Shakespeare's language, his life, his theater, a "Modern Perspective," and further reading. There is a wealth of scholarship embedded in these wonderful books, and I make it a point to read them cover to cover before embarking on a play-directing project. At the very least, it is a good idea for any adult who intends to direct a Shakespeare play with a group of students to go through the explanatory notes that appear on the pages facing the text. These explanatory notes are an indispensable "translation tool."

The best way to get students to understand what Shakespeare's words mean is to ask them what they think they mean. Students have their own associations with the words and with how they sound and feel. The best ideas on how to perform Shakespeare often come directly from the students, not from anybody else's notion. If a student has an idea or feeling about a word or passage, and it resonates with her emotionally, physically, or spiritually, then Shakespeare's words can be a vehicle for her feelings. That can result in some powerful performances!

I make it my job as director to read the explanatory notes in the Folger text, but I make it clear to the students that almost "anything goes" when trying to understand Shakespeare. There are no wrong interpretations. Students have their own experiences, with some shared and some uniquely their own. If someone has an association with the phrase "canker-blossom," or if the words make that student or his character feel or act a certain way, then that is the "right" way to decipher it.

I encourage the students to refer to the Folger text's explanatory notes and to keep a pocket dictionary handy. Young actors must attach some meaning to every word or line they recite. If I feel an actor is glossing over a word, I will stop him and ask him what he is saying. If he doesn't know, we will figure it out together as a group.

PROCESS VS. PRODUCT

The process of learning Shakespeare by performing one of his plays is more important than whether everybody remembers his lines or whether somebody misses a cue or an entrance. But my Teaching Artist residencies have always had the end goal of a public performance for about 200 other students, so naturally the performance starts to take precedence over the process somewhere around dress rehearsal in the students' minds. It is my job to make sure the actors are prepared— otherwise they will remember the embarrassing moment of a public mistake and not the glorious triumph of owning a Shakespeare play.

In one of my earlier years of play directing, I was sitting in the audience as one of my narrators stood frozen on stage for at least a minute, trying to remember her opening line. I started scrambling in my backpack below my seat for a script, at last prompting her from the audience. Despite her fine performance, that embarrassing moment is all she remembered from the whole experience. Since then I have made sure to assign at least one person to prompt from backstage if necessary. Additionally, I inform the entire cast that if somebody is dying alone out there, it is okay to rescue him or her with an offstage prompt.

There is always a certain amount of stage fright that will accompany a performance, especially a public one for an unfamiliar audience. As a director, I live with stage fright as well, even though I am not appearing on stage. The only antidote to this is work and preparation. If a young actor is struggling with her lines, I make sure to arrange for a session where we run lines over the telephone. I try to set up a buddy system so that students can run lines with their peers, and this often works well. But if somebody does not have a "buddy," I will personally make the time to help out myself. As I assure my students from the outset, I am not going to let them fail or embarrass themselves. They need an experienced leader. And if the leader has experience in teaching but not in directing Shakespeare, then he needs this book!

It is a good idea to culminate in a public performance, as opposed to an in-class project, even if it is only for another classroom. Student actors want to show their newfound Shakespearian thespian skills to an outside group, and this goal motivates them to do a good job. In that respect, "product" is important. Another wonderful bonus to performing a play is that it is a unifying group effort. Students learn teamwork. They learn to give focus to another actor when he is speaking, and to play off of other characters. I like to end each performance with the entire cast reciting a passage in unison. This is a powerful ending, one that reaffirms the unity of the group.

SEEING SHAKESPEARE PERFORMED

It is very helpful for young actors to see Shakespeare performed by a group of professionals, whether they are appearing live on stage (preferable but not always possible) or on film. Because an entire play can take up two or more full class periods, time may be an issue. I am fortunate because thanks to a local foundation that underwrites theater education in the schools, I have been able to take my school groups to a Folger Theatre matinee of the play that they are performing. I always pick a play that is being performed locally that season. But not all group leaders are that lucky. Fortunately, there is the Internet, specifically YouTube. A quick YouTube search for "Shakespeare" can unearth thousands of results, many appropriate for the classroom.

The first "Hamlet" result showed an 18-year-old African-American actor on the streets of Camden, New Jersey, delivering a riveting performance of Hamlet's "The play's the thing." The second clip was from *Cat Head Theatre,* an animation of cats performing Hamlet. Of course, YouTube boasts not just alley cats and feline thespians, but also clips by true legends of the stage, such as John Gielgud and Richard Burton. These clips can be saved and shown in classrooms, providing useful inspiration.

One advantage of the amazing variety of clips available on YouTube is that students can witness the wide range of interpretations for any given scene, speech, or character in Shakespeare, thus freeing them from any preconceived notion that there is a "right" way to do it. Furthermore, modern interpretations of the Bard may appeal to those who are put off by the "thees and thous" of Elizabethan speech.

By seeing Shakespeare performed either live or on film, students are able to hear the cadence, rhythm, vocal dynamics, and pronunciation of the language, and they can appreciate the life that other actors breathe into the characters. They get to see the story told dramatically, which inspires them to tell their own version.

PUTTING IT ALL TOGETHER

THE STEPS

After a few sessions of theater games to warm up the group, it's time to begin the process of casting the play. Each play cutting in *The 30-Minute Shakespeare* series includes a cast list and a sample program, demonstrating which parts have been divided. Cast size is generally between twelve and thirty students, with major roles frequently assigned to more than one performer. In other words, one student may play Juliet in the first scene, another in the second scene, and yet another in the third. This will distribute the parts evenly so that there is no "star of the show." Furthermore, this prevents actors from being burdened with too many lines. If I have an actor who is particularly talented or enthusiastic, I will give her a bigger role. It is important to go with the grain—one cast member's enthusiasm can be contagious.

I provide the performer of each shared role with a similar head-piece and/or cape, so that the audience can keep track of the characters. When there are sets of twins, I try to use blue shirts and red shirts, so that the audience has at least a fighting chance of figuring it out! Other than these costume consistencies, I rely on the text and the audience's observance to sort out the doubling of characters. Generally, the audience can follow because we are telling the story.

Some participants are shy and do not wish to speak at all on stage. To these students I assign non-speaking parts and technical roles such as sound operator and stage manager. However, I always get everybody on stage at some point, even if it is just for the final group speech, because I want every group member to experience what it is like to be on a stage as part of an ensemble.

CASTING THE PLAY

Young people can be self-conscious and nervous with "formal" auditions, especially if they have little or no acting experience.

I conduct what I call an "informal" audition process. I hand out a questionnaire asking students if there is any particular role that they desire, whether they play a musical instrument. To get a feel for them as people, I also ask them to list one or two hobbies or interests. Occasionally this will inform my casting decisions. If someone can juggle, and the play has the part of a Fool, that skill may come in handy. Dancing or martial arts abilities can also be applied to roles.

For the auditions, I do not use the cut script. I have students stand and read from the Folger edition of the complete text in order to hear how they fare with the longer passages. I encourage them to breathe and carry their vocal energy all the way to the end of a long line of text. I also urge them to play with diction, projection, modulation, and dynamics, elements of speech that we have worked on in our vocal warm-ups and theater games.

I base my casting choices largely on reading ability, vocal strength, and enthusiasm for the project. If someone has requested a particular role, I try to honor that request. I explain that even with a small part, an actor can create a vivid character that adds a lot to the play. Wide variations in personality types can be utilized: if there are two students cast as Romeo, one brooding and one effusive, I try to put the more brooding Romeo in an early lovelorn scene, and place the effusive Romeo in the balcony scene. Occasionally one gets lucky, and the doubling of characters provides a way to match personality types with different aspects of a character's personality. But also be aware of the potential serendipity of non-traditional casting. For example, I have had one of the smallest students in the class play a powerful Othello. True power comes from within!

Generally, I have more females than males in a class, so women are more likely (and more willing) to play male characters than vice versa.

Rare is the high school boy who is brave enough to play a female character, which is unfortunate because it can reap hilarious results.

GET OUTSIDE HELP

Every time there is a fight scene in one of the plays I am directing, I call on my friend Michael Tolaydo, a professional actor and theater professor at St. Mary's College, who is an expert in all aspects of theater, including fight choreography. Not only does Michael stage the fight, but he does so in a way that furthers the action of the play, highlighting character's traits and bringing out the best in the student actors. Fight choreography must be done by an expert or somebody could get hurt. In the absence of such help, super slow-motion fights are always a safe bet and can be quite effective, especially when accompanied by a soundtrack on the boom box.

During dress rehearsals I invite my friend Hilary Kacser. a Washington-area actor and dialect coach for two decades. Because I bring her in late in the rehearsal process, I have her direct her comments to me, which I then filter and relay to the cast. This avoids confusing the cast with a second set of directions. This caveat only applies to general directorial comments from outside visitors. Comments on specific artistic disciplines such as dance, music, and stage combat can come from the outside experts themselves.

If you work in a school, you might have helpful resources within your own building, such as a music or dance teacher who could contribute their expertise to a scene. If nobody is available in your school, try seeking out a member of the local professional theater. Many local performing artists will be glad to help, and the students are usually thrilled to have a visit from a professional performer.

LET STUDENTS BRING THEMSELVES INTO THE PLAY

The best ideas often come from the students themselves. If a young actor has a notion of how to play a scene, I will always give that idea a try. In a rehearsal of *Henry IV, Part 1,* one traveler jumped into the other's arms when they were robbed. It got a huge laugh. This was something that they did on instinct. We kept that bit for the performance, and it worked wonderfully.

As a director, you have to foster an environment in which that kind of spontaneity can occur. The students have to feel safe to experiment. In the same production of *Henry IV,* Falstaff and Hal invented a little fist bump "secret handshake" to use in the battle scene. The students were having fun and bringing parts of themselves into the play. Shakespeare himself would have approved. When possible I try to err on the side of fun because if the young actors are having fun, then they will commit themselves to the project. The beauty of the language, the story, the characters, and the pathos will follow.

There is a balance to be achieved here, however. In that same production of *Henry IV, Part 1,* the student who played Bardolph was having a great time with her character. She carried a leather wineskin around and offered it up to the other characters in the tavern. It was a prop with which she developed a comic relationship. At the end of our thirty-minute *Henry IV, Part 1,* I added a scene from *Henry IV, Part 2* as a coda: The new King Henry V (formerly Falstaff's drinking and carousing buddy Hal) rejects Falstaff, banishing him from within ten miles of the King. It is a sad and sobering moment, one of the most powerful in the play.

But at the performance, in the middle of the King's rejection speech (played by a female student, and her only speech), Bardolph offered her flask to King Henry and got a big laugh, thus not only upstaging the King but also undermining the seriousness and poignancy of the whole scene. She did not know any better; she was bringing herself to the character as I had been encouraging her to do. But it was inappropriate, and in subsequent seasons, if I foresaw something like that happening as an individual joyfully occupied a character, I attempted to prevent it. Some things we cannot predict. Now I make sure to issue a statement warning against changing any of the blocking on show day, and to watch out for upstaging one's peers.

FOUR FORMS OF ENGAGEMENT: VOCAL, EMOTIONAL, PHYSICAL, AND INTELLECTUAL

When directing a Shakespeare play with a group of students, I always start with the words themselves because the words have the power to engage the emotions, mind, and body. Also, I start with the words in action, as in the previously mentioned exercise, "Positive and Negative Salutations." Students become physically engaged; their bodies react to the images the words evoke. The words have the power to trigger a switch in both the teller and the listener, eliciting both an emotional and physical reaction. I have never heard a student utter the line "Fie! Fie! You counterfeit, you puppet you!" without seeing him change before my eyes. His spine stiffens, his eyes widen, and his fingers point menacingly.

Having used Shakespeare's words to engage the students emotionally and physically, one can then return to the text for a more reflective discussion of what the words mean to us personally. I always make sure to leave at least a few class periods open for discussion of the text, line by line, to ensure that students understand intellectually what they feel viscerally. The advantage to a performance-based teaching of Shakespeare is that by engaging students vocally, emotionally, and physically, it is then much easier to engage them intellectually because they are invested in the words, the characters, and the story. We always start on our feet, and later we sit and talk.

SIX ELEMENTS OF DRAMA: PLOT, CHARACTER, THEME, DICTION, MUSIC, AND SPECTACLE

Over two thousand years ago, Aristotle's *Poetics* outlined six elements of drama, in order of importance: Plot, Character, Theme, Diction, Music, and Spectacle. Because Shakespeare was foremost a playwright, it is helpful to take a brief look at these six elements as they relate to directing a Shakespeare play in the classroom.

PLOT (ACTION)

To Aristotle, plot was the most important element. One of the pur-
poses of *The 30-Minute Shakespeare* is to provide a script that tells
Shakespeare's stories, as opposed to concentrating on one scene. In a
thirty-minute edit of a Shakespeare play, some plot elements are necessarily omitted. For the sake of a full understanding of the characters'
relationships and motivations, it is helpful to make short plot sum-
maries of each scene so that students are aware of their characters' arcs
throughout the play. The scene descriptions in the Folger editions are
sufficient to fill in the plot holes. Students can read the descriptions
aloud during class time to ensure that the story is clear and that no
plot elements are neglected. Additionally, there are one-page charts
in the Folger editions of *Shakespeare Set Free,* indicating characters'
relations graphically, with lines connecting families and factions to
give students a visual representation of what can often be complex
interrelationships, particularly in Shakespeare's history plays.

Young actors love action. That is why *The 30-Minute Shakespeare*
includes dynamic blocking (stage direction) that allows students to tell
the story in a physically dramatic fashion. Characters' movements on
the stage are always motivated by the text itself.

CHARACTER

I consider myself a facilitator and a director more than an acting
teacher. I want the students' understanding of their characters to spring
from the text and the story. From there, I encourage them to consider
how their character might talk, walk, stand, sit, eat, and drink. I also
urge students to consider characters' motivations, objectives, and
relationships, and I will ask pointed questions to that end during
the rehearsal process. I try not to show the students how I would
perform a scene, but if no ideas are forthcoming from anybody in
the class, I will suggest a minimum of two possibilities for how the
character might respond.

At times students may want more guidance and examples. Over thirteen years of directing plays in the classroom, I have wavered between wanting all the ideas to come from the students, and deciding that I need to be more of a "director," telling them what I would like to see them doing. It is a fine line, but in recent years I have decided that if I don't see enough dynamic action or characterization, I will step in and "direct" more. But I always make sure to leave room for students to bring themselves into the characters because their own ideas are invariably the best.

THEME (THOUGHTS, IDEAS)

In a typical English classroom, theme will be a big topic for discussion of a Shakespeare play. Using a performance-based method of teaching Shakespeare, an understanding of the play's themes develops from "mining the text" and exploring Shakespeare's words and his story. If the students understand what they are saying and how that relates to their characters and the overall story, the plays' themes will emerge clearly. We always return to the text itself. There are a number of elegant computer programs, such as www.wordle.net, that will count the number of recurring words in a passage and illustrate them graphically. For example, if the word "jealousy" comes up more than any other word in *Othello*, it will appear in a larger font. Seeing the words displayed by size in this way can offer up illuminating insights into the interaction between words in the text and the play's themes. Your computer-minded students might enjoy searching for such tidbits. There are more internet tools and websites in the Additional Resources section at the back of this book.

I cannot overstress the importance of acting out the play in understanding its themes. By embodying the roles of Othello and Iago and reciting their words, students do not simply comprehend the themes intellectually, but understand them kinesthetically, physically, and emotionally. They are essentially *living* the characters' jealousy, pride, and feelings about race. The themes of appearance vs.

reality, good vs. evil, honesty, misrepresentation, and self-knowledge (or lack thereof) become physically felt as well as intellectually understood. Performing Shakespeare delivers a richer understanding than that which comes from just reading the play. Students can now relate the characters' conflicts to their own struggles.

DICTION (LANGUAGE)

If I had to cite one thing I would like my actors to take from their experience of performing a play by William Shakespeare, it is an appreciation and understanding of the beauty of Shakespeare's language. The language is where it all begins and ends. Shakespeare's stories are dramatic, his characters are rich and complex, and his settings are exotic and fascinating, but it is through his language that these all achieve their richness. This leads me to spend more time on language than on any other element of the performance.

Starting with daily vocal warm-ups, many of them using parts of the script or other Shakespearean passages, I consistently emphasize the importance of the words. Young actors often lack experience in speaking clearly and projecting their voices outward, so in addition to comprehension, I emphasize projection, diction, breathing, pacing, dynamics, coloring of words, and vocal energy. *Theatre Games for Young Performers* contains many effective vocal exercises, as does the Folger's *Shakespeare Set Free* series. Consistent emphasis on all aspects of Shakespeare's language, especially on how to speak it effectively, is the most important element to any Shakespeare performance with a young cast.

MUSIC

A little music can go a long way in setting a mood for a thirty-minute Shakespeare play. I usually open the show with a short passage of music to set the tone. Thirty seconds of music played on a boom box operated by a student can provide a nice introduction to the play, create an atmosphere for the audience, and give the actors a sense of place and feeling.

iTunes is a good starting point for choosing your music. Typing in "Shakespeare" or "Hamlet" or "jealousy" (if you are going for a theme) will result in an excellent selection of aural performance enhancers at the very reasonable price of ninety-nine cents each (or free of charge, see Additional Resources section). Likewise, fight sounds, foreboding sounds, weather sounds (rain, thunder), trumpet sounds, etc. are all readily available online at affordable cost. I typically include three sound cues in a play, just enough to enhance but not overpower a production. The boom box operator sits on the far right or left of the stage, not backstage, so he can see the action. This also has the added benefit of having somebody out there with a script, capable of prompting in a pinch.

SPECTACLE

Aristotle considered spectacle the least important aspect of drama. Students tend to be surprised at this since we are used to being bombarded with production values on TV and video, often at the expense of substance. In my early days of putting on student productions, I would find myself hamstrung by my own ambitions in the realm of scenic design.

A simple bench or two chairs set on the stage are sufficient. The sense of "place" can be achieved through language and acting. Simple set dressing, a few key props, and some tasteful, emblematic costume pieces will go a long way toward providing all the "spectacle" you need.

In the stage directions to the plays in *The 30-Minute Shakespeare* series, I make frequent use of two large pillars stage left and right at the Folger Shakespeare Library's Elizabethan Theatre. I also have characters frequently entering and exiting from "stage rear." Your stage will have a different layout. Take a good look at the performing space you will be using and see if there are any elements that can be incorporated into your own stage directions. Is there a balcony? Can characters enter from the audience? (Make sure that they can get there from backstage, unless you want them waiting in the lobby until their entrance, which may be impractical.) If possible, make sure to rehearse in that space a few times to fix any technical issues and perhaps discover a few fun staging variations that will add pizzazz and dynamics to your own show.

The real spectacle is in the telling of the tale. Wooden swords are handy for characters that need them. Students should be warned at the outset that playing with swords outside of the scene is verboten. Letters, moneybags, and handkerchiefs should all have plentiful duplicates kept in a small prop box, as well as with a stage manager, because they tend to disappear in the hands of adolescents. After every rehearsal and performance, I recommend you personally sweep the rehearsal or performance area immediately for stray props. It is amazing what gets left behind.

Ultimately, the performances are about language and human drama, not set pieces, props, and special effects. Fake blood, glitter, glass, and liquids have no place on the stage; they are a recipe for disaster, or, at the very least, a big mess. On the other hand, the props that are employed can often be used effectively to convey character, as in Bardolph's aforementioned relationship with his wineskin.

PITFALLS AND SOLUTIONS

Putting on a play in a high school classroom is not easy. There are problems with enthusiasm, attitude, attention, and line memorization, to name a few. As anybody who has directed a play will tell you, it is always darkest before the dawn. My experience is that after one or two days of utter despair just before the play goes up, show day breaks and the play miraculously shines. To quote a recurring gag in one of my favorite movies, *Shakespeare in Love*: "It's a mystery."

ENTHUSIASM, FRUSTRATION, AND DISCIPLINE

Bring the enthusiasm yourself. Feed on the energy of the eager students, and others will pick up on that. Keep focused on the task at hand. Arrive prepared. Enthusiasm comes as you make headway. Ultimately, it helps to remind the students that a play is fun. I try to focus on the positive attributes of the students, rather than the ones that drive me crazy. This is easier said than done, but it is important. One season, I yelled at the group two days in a row. On day two of yelling, they tuned me out, and it took me a while to win them back. I learned my lesson; since then I've tried not to raise my voice out of anger or frustration. As I grow older and more mature, it is important for me to lead by example. It has been years since I yelled at a student group. If I am disappointed in their work or their behavior, I will express my disenchantment in words, speaking from the heart as somebody who cares about them and cares about our performance and our experience together. I find that fundamentally, young people want to please, to do well, and to be liked. If there is a serious discipline problem, I will hand it over to the regular classroom teacher, the administrator, or the parent.

LINE MEMORIZATION

Students may have a hard time memorizing lines. In these cases, see if you can pair them up with a "buddy" and existing friend who will run lines with them in person or over the phone after school. If students do not have such a "buddy," I volunteer to run lines with them myself. If serious line memorization problems arise that cannot be solved through work, then two students can switch parts if it is early enough in the rehearsal process. For doubled roles, the scene with fewer lines can go to the actor who is having memorization problems. Additionally, a few passages or lines can be cut. Again, it is important to address these issues early. Later cuts become more problematic as other actors have already memorized their cues. I have had to do late cuts about twice in thirteen years. While they have gotten us out of jams, it is best to assess early whether a student will have line memorization problems, and deal with the problem sooner rather than later.

In production, always keep several copies of the script backstage, as well as cheat sheets indicating cues, entrances, and scene changes. Make a prop list, indicating props for each scene, as well as props that are the responsibility of individual actors. Direct the Stage Manager and an Assistant Stage Manager to keep track of these items, and on show days, personally double-check if you can.

In thirteen years of preparing an inner-city public high school English class for a public performance on a field trip to the Folger Secondary School Shakespeare Festival, my groups and I have been beset by illness, emotional turmoil, discipline problems, stage fright, adolescent angst, midlife crises (not theirs), and all manner of other emergencies, including acts of God and nature. Despite the difficulties and challenges inherent in putting on a Shakespeare play with a group of young people, one amazing fact stands out in my experience. Here is how many times a student has been absent for show day: Zero. Somehow, everybody has always made it to the show, and the show has gone on. How can this be? It's a mystery.

✳ PERFORMANCE NOTES:
THE COMEDY OF ERRORS

I directed this performance of *The Comedy of Errors* in 2004. These notes are the result of my own review of the performance video. They are not intended to be the "definitive" performance notes for all productions of *The Comedy of Errors*. Your production will be unique to you and your cast. That is the magic of live theater. What is interesting about these notes is that many of the performance details I mention were not part of the original stage directions. They either emerged spontaneously on performance day or were developed by students in rehearsal after the stage directions had been written into the script. Some of these pieces of stage business work like a charm. Others fall flat. My favorites are the ones that arise directly from the students themselves, and demonstrate a union between actor and character, as if that individual had become a vehicle for the character he is playing. To witness a fourteen-year old young man "become" Egeon as Shakespeare's words leave his mouth is a memorable moment indeed.

SCENE 1 (ACT I, SCENE I)

Like many of the plays I have directed for the Folger Library Student Shakespeare Festival, this thirty-minute production of *The Comedy of Errors* has simple staging. We create a sense of place and character using our bodies and our words, plus a few well-placed musical cues. Courtly music at the top of Scene 1 sets the mood, and helps define where we are (i.e., at the Duke's palace). Duke Solinus sits on the throne. Egeon is hooded and bound with his hands behind his back, kneeling. Thus with a few props, costumes, and staging ideas we create a strong visual image that contributes to painting the scene, the relationship, and the status of the characters. The actress playing Duke of Solinus wanted to play her character as a female, so we changed the character from "Duke" to "Duchess," which added an interesting dynamic to the play and inspired me to experiment with gender switching in subsequent performances.

During Egeon's speech about why he came to Ephesus, we create another tableau. This one greatly enhances the verbal exposition and makes it clear to the audience what to expect. Especially in a confusing comedy of mistaken identity, if the audience is not clear on the story from the outset, they will remain confused, which will detract from their enjoyment of the play. If the audience understands the story, they can then relax and enjoy the language and the characterizations.

This particular vignette introduces the two sets of twins. Each Antipholus wears the same color shirt and hat, and each Dromio wears a different color, making it easier for the audience to follow them as the comedy continues. Each set of twins holds a pole horizontally, with the two poles forming a line to represent one mast. On the line "our ship was splitted in the midst," the pole splits, and the two pairs of twins separate, with one half of each pair exiting stage right and the other half stage left.

This speech by Egeon is an important piece of plot explanation; the actor should therefore slow down and color his words. Simple physical gestures can also enhance the players' line deliveries. The "throat slit" gesture can add punch to the Duke's line "for thou art doomed to die." Young actors benefit from having particular descriptive movements accompany words or phrases. It gives them confidence and helps them memorize their lines, since there is a mnemonic benefit to pairing words with actions.

SCENE 2 (ACT I, SCENE II)

The ninth-grade young woman who played Antipholus of Syracuse in our 2004 production of *The Comedy of Errors* had a nice clear voice accompanied by crisp gestures. Her scene with Dromio of Ephesus is the first of many mistaken identity scenes, and it sets the tone for subsequent hilarious errors. In this scene, the actress playing Antipholus of Syracuse takes great pleasure in beating Dromio of Ephesus with her character's hat. Fortunately, the performer portraying Dromio also took joy in cowering on his back, covering his head with his hands to avoid the beating.

For the scene to succeed, the person being beaten must be the one in control. This is broad physical comedy, and it benefits from expansive exaggerated movements from the actors. The farther they take the physical comedy, through commitment to big movements and silliness, the more fun they have with it, and the audience picks up on the merriment.

How do we take it farther? One simple exercise is to play a theatrical moment four different ways: small, normal, bigger, and over-the-top. "Small" entails purposefully saying one's line in an almost inaudible whisper with little body movement. Most participants agree that there is not much sense in delivering a line that the audience can't hear.

"Normal" means "as if one were sitting in a room talking." The actor makes no additional effort to project or enunciate, nor does she try to emote.

When an actor recites a line of Shakespeare in "normal" mode, other players usually find this lacking too. Sometimes I point out to them that this is actually what I am seeing and hearing when they think they are performing at the next level: "bigger."

"Bigger" implies a level of exaggeration or stylization that is a hallmark of stage acting: chewing the words, holding a gesture or pose slightly larger and longer than usual, and projecting as if one were trying to reach the back row. It also calls for a greater vocal range: the words take on a more sing-song quality, the pitch gets higher and lower, and the facial expressions are more pronounced. If you are lucky, your actors will achieve this third level in their performance: "bigger." The final level is the most useful in comedy, but also helpful with beginning actors in any genre: "over the top."

In "over the top," I encourage my thespians to throw caution to the wind and see just how big, loud, exaggerated, and ridiculous they can be, without regard to whether it makes sense for the scene. I am essentially asking them to go beyond their perceived limits of decorum. I assure them that it is impossible for them to overact or overemphasize in this exercise. I am asking for systematic and purposeful breaking of boundaries. This is where it gets interesting, because frequently what young actors give me at this stage is exactly what I want! Nobody ever goes too far, and what many young actors consider "over the top" is actually what I see as the proper level of exaggeration for a silly comedy. The most important lesson to be derived from this exercise is that there is a great range of possibilities and we often don't know what the scope is until we experiment with stretching our limits. This exercise can be applied to just vocals, as well as speech combined with movement.

SCENE 3 (ACT II, SCENE II)

The narrator begins the scene by explaining the increasingly convoluted circumstances surrounding the two sets of twins, finally exclaiming, "Confused? Good. So are they!" During rehearsal, we added, "So am I!" as a coda, which got a laugh, partly because it gave the narrator an identity and a personality. Even small roles, in this case a role with no character name, can have charisma and add to the dramatic life of the play.

In this scene, we repeat the comic bit of Antipholus repeatedly striking Dromio with his hat, only this time they chase each other around the bench. Dromio also slides under the bench to try to avoid being beaten, thus taking the physical comedy one step farther.

Dromio ends up with the hat, and proceeds to hit Antipholus with it. By having Antipholus beat Dromio with his hat for a second time, we establish a physical vocabulary for the comedy. Repetition enhances humor. Having Dromio turn the tables by beating Antipholus with the hat adds a twist to the comedy: the element of surprise. I missed an opportunity here to repeat this comic bit a third time, with yet another twist. Doing so would have gotten a bigger laugh than before, due to comedy's rule of three. Perhaps at the very end of the play as the two sets of twins recited the line "we came into the world like brother and brother…" they could have given one another one more whack on the head with the hat, to put a cap on the comedy!

As Adriana and Luciana enter, Dromio and Antipholus are no longer fighting; they are on the same team. Dromio nudges Antipholus to talk to this woman who believes she is his wife. In this scene, Luciana demonstrates her no-nonsense character with physical poses: crossed arms and defiant posture. On each name she calls Dromio, she pokes him in the chest: "Thou drone," (poke) "thou snail," (poke) "thou slug," (poke) "thou sot," (poke poke poke), ultimately backing poor Dromio up against the wall. These physical moves work wonders in accentuating Shakespeare's words and increasing the audience laughter.

When Antipholus exclaims "And in the mist at all adventure go," he raises his sword high and jogs out enthusiastically, following the ladies. Simple, effective blocking and physical gestures, combined with actor enthusiasm, helps players and audience alike gain a better understanding of Shakespeare's text, characters, and relationships. The result is a merry play!

SCENE 4 (ACT III, SCENE II)

To open this scene, we repeat the comic bit from the top of Scene 3. The narrator tries to clarify recent plot developments in a couple of sentences, concluding her speech with "Are you following this? Don't worry about it. Neither am I." Originally I had the narrator saying, "Neither are they," but "Neither am I" works well because it gives brings the narrator into the story and gives her a personality. This is the second instance of narrator confusion. I remembered to employ the comedy "rule of three" this time, by having the narrator reiterate her confusion for the last time at the beginning of Scene 5.

Antipholus of Syracuse's romantic bids towards Luciana in this scene are staged like a dance: She sits on the bench, and then he sits on the bench next to her. She moves down the bench; then he moves down the bench next to her. He tries to put his arm around her, then she moves away suddenly, and he falls on his face on the bench. Again, by introducing a change to the dance on the third move, we have set up a pattern, and then broken it on the third endeavor, thus surprising the audience into laughter!

Dromio of Syracuse's entrance is fast and furious. He flails his arms and legs breathlessly, and his wild eyes are bugging out. The actress playing Dromio in our 2004 show had a wiry build, with long arms and legs, and her frantic physicalizations provided a nice contrast to Antipholus of Syracuse's portly physique and composed, tranquil demeanor. In this instance, it was just serendipity that the young lady playing Dromio was thin, sinewy, and naturally energetic, while the young man portraying Antipholus was stocky and inherently calm. Sometimes the actors' body types and mannerisms line up to produce a comic counterpoint.

There is an understandable temptation to "go with the grain," using players' native attributes to dictate how to play the scene. It is a good practice to experiment with different ways of performing a moment, sometimes purposefully going against the grain. In this scene, for example, Dromio has many options on how to interpret his role. He could play it frantic and frightened, as he did in this scene, but he could also be convulsing in laughter, retching with disgust, angry, confused, etc. Even if you don't end up choosing that interpretation, the alternate takes on the moment often yield revelations about the character and the text.

By experimenting with different ways of performing the text, we discover that although Shakespeare's words remain unchanged, our dramatic portrayals often lead widely divergent results, which in turn result in new and exciting interpretations of the play.

SCENE 5 (ACT V, SCENE I)

The narrator begins the final scene by trying to explain some plot points, and finishes her speech with the explanation "There is more confusion. We are praying for a happy ending." This gets a good laugh, as the third joke in a series often does.

Antipholus of Syracuse really gets in the merchant's face, and appears to be on the verge of drawing his sword, which ups the ante for the scene. In a comedy, it helps to have moments where the story could take a turn in the other direction, towards violence or tragedy. In general, playing the characters' emotions and conflicts earnestly rather than playing them for laughs will reap the biggest comedic rewards. This way the humor comes from the characters, the language, the action, and the circumstances as they unfold to the audience. We trust that by believing in these elements, the humor will emerge!

The actress playing Adriana had a strong comic personality and physical poise. When she exclaimed "Aye me; it is my husband," she said it straight out towards the audience. Her expression was deadpan, but her eyes were bugging out, and the audience could not help laughing. This Adriana was committed to audience laughter, and she achieved it by playing her character straight, but with a noticeable edge or intensity that allowed the audience to both sympathize with her plight, but also laugh at its absurdity.

The ninth-grade actress who played Adriana had a good grasp of character dynamics. As Adriana, she was self-assured and confident, but as soon as the more powerful Duke appeared on the scene, she was earnestly contrite, bowing her head in deference. By portraying these two sides of the same person, depending on the status of her theatrical counterpart, this young actress was able to present a fully rounded character, while still retaining the silliness necessary for comedy. Both her confident self and her contrite personage were exaggerated just enough to imbue her role with the ingredients for audience laughter. Playing traits to extremes is a great way to get to the heart of a comedy. Underneath the exaggeration, there has to be earnestness for the humor to work its magic.

Egeon's reunion with his sons is a potentially poignant theatrical moment, if played with feeling. The encounter is sweet when contrasted with the sorrow that preceded it. How does a young actor play the joy of a tearful reunion with long-lost sons, while expressing the sorrow and fear that accompanied their missing years? The best place to start is in Shakespeare's words themselves:

> "Oh grief hath changed me since you saw me last,
> And careful hours with time's deformed hand
> Have written strange defeatures in my face:
> But tell me yet, dost thou not know my voice?"

By coloring these words and letting them express Egeon's emotions, the sad beauty emerges. Actors should focus on the meaning and feeling of the words, and let Shakespeare's story tell itself through them. There are numerous acting techniques and staging devices that enhance the production, but we must not forget to return to the beauty and power of William Shakespeare's words. Rather than rushing through the speeches, actors must color individual words, and really let them hang in the air, only to fall evocatively on listeners' ears.

When Adriana exclaims, "I see two husbands, or mine eyes deceive me," her head swings back and forth between the two Antipholuses like a bobble head doll, to great comic effect. At this point near the close of the play, there are many actors on stage. Optimal staging places the Duke in the middle, center stage, and the two sets of twins on either side. This produces the greatest visibility and comprehension, as the comedy's mysteries are revealed and the errors are corrected.

Both Antipholuses and Dromios say the final line once together, followed by the whole cast in unison:

"We came into the world like brother and brother
And now let's go hand in hand, not one before the other!"

With this merry exclamation, *The Comedy of Errors* ends. Live theater is magical. It is the most dynamic form of entertainment available to us. There is nothing like the interchange between actors and audience, that vibrant energy that is created in the theater. *The Comedy of Errors* is one of Shakespeare's most beloved comedies, and we are fortunate to be able to continue bringing it to life, especially with young performers who can give it the vitality it deserves.

✳ *THE COMEDY OF ERRORS:* SET AND PROP LIST

SET PIECES:

Throne
Chair
Bench

PROPS:

SCENE 1:

Handcuffs for Egeon
Two thick dowel rods or poles for ship mast

SCENE 2:

Bag of money for First Merchant to give to Dromio of Syracuse

SCENE 4:

Gold chain for Angelo

SCENE 5:

Swords for Antipholus and First Merchant
Rope for Egeon
Bag of money for Antipholus of Epheseus

BENJAMIN BANNEKER SENIOR HIGH SCHOOL *presents*

The Comedy of Errors

By William Shakespeare

Performed by the 6th period Ninth Grade English Class

Instructor: Mr. Leo Bowman | Guest Director: Mr. Nick Newlin

CAST OF CHARACTERS:

Scene 1:
Outside the Duchess's Palace
Narrator: Taryn Cobb
Egeon: Samuel Collins, Jr.
Duchess: Sharde Curley
Jailer: Jimmy Gomez

Scene 2:
The Mart
Narrator: Jenny Gonzalez
First Merchant: Brittany Coote
Antipholus of Syracuse: Tiera King
Dromio of Syracuse: Charles Garland
Dromio of Ephesus: Andre Davis

Scene 3:
Outside Antipholus of Ephesus's house
Narrator: Brittany Coote
Antipholus of Syracuse: Duane Fon
Dromio of Syracuse: Terrill Dongmo
Adriana: Doneisha Falwell
Luciana: Regina Graves

Scene 4:
Outside Antipholus of Ephesus's house
Narrator: Ashley Craig
Luciana: Taryn Cobb
Antipholus of Syracuse: Melvin Glymph
Dromio of Sytracuse: Stephanie Gibson
Angelo: Jenny Gonzalez

Scene 5:
A street before a Priory
Narrator: Rachel Dunlap
2nd Merchant: Ashley Craig
Servant: Rachel Dunlap
Antipholus of Syracuse: Ameer Dyson
Dromio of Syracuse: Charles Garland
Adriana: Alektra Daniels
Luciana: Taryn Cobb
Duchess: Cheyenne Glenn
Egeon: Ola Canty
Abbess/Emilia: Rachelle Green
Antipholus of Ephesus: Brannon Floyd
Dromio of Ephesus: Andre Davis
Angelo: Jimmy Gomez

Stage Manager: Ngoc Duong
Technical Director: Adrian Robinson
Costumes and Props: Kristel Taylor

*"I to the world am like a drop of water
That in the ocean seeks another drop..."*
Antipholus of Syracuse

ADDITIONAL RESOURCES

SHAKESPEARE

Shakespeare Set Free: Teaching Romeo and Juliet, Macbeth and a Midsummer Night's Dream
Peggy O'Brien, Ed., Teaching Shakespeare Institute
Washington Square Press
New York, 1993

Shakespeare Set Free: Teaching Hamlet and Henry IV, Part 1
Peggy O'Brien, Ed., Teaching Shakespeare Institute
Washington Square Press
New York, 1994

Shakespeare Set Free: Teaching Twelfth Night and Othello
Peggy O'Brien, Ed., Teaching Shakespeare Institute
Washington Square Press
New York, 1995

The *Shakespeare Set Free* series is an invaluable resource with lesson plans, activites, handouts, and excellent suggestions for rehearsing and performing Shakespeare plays in a classroom setting.

ShakesFear and How to Cure It!
Ralph Alan Cohen
Prestwick House, Inc.
Delaware, 2006

The Friendly Shakespeare: A Thoroughly Painless Guide to the Best of the Bard
Norrie Epstein
Penguin Books
New York, 1994

Brush Up Your Shakespeare!
Michael Macrone
Cader Books
New York, 1990

Shakespeare's Insults: Educating Your Wit
Wayne F. Hill and Cynthia J. Ottchen
Three Rivers Press
New York, 1991

Practical Approaches to Teaching Shakespeare
Peter Reynolds
Oxford University Press
New York, 1991

Scenes From Shakespeare:
A Workbook for Actors
Robin J. Holt
McFarland and Co.
London, 1988

THEATER AND PERFORMANCE

Impro: Improvisation and the Theatre
Keith Johnstone
Routledge Books
London, 1982

A Dictionary of Theatre Anthropology:
The Secret Art of the Performer
Eugenio Barba and Nicola Savarese
Routledge
London, 1991

THEATER GAMES

Theatre Games for Young Performers
Maria C. Novelly
Meriwether Publishing
Colorado, 1990

Improvisation for the Theater
Viola Spolin
Northwestern University Press
Illinois, 1983

Theater Games for Rehearsal:
A Director's Handbook
Viola Spolin
Northwestern University Press
Illinois, 1985

101 Theatre Games for Drama
Teachers, Classroom Teachers
& Directors
Mila Johansen
Players Press Inc.
California, 1994

PLAY DIRECTING

Theater and the Adolescent Actor:
Building a Successful School Program
Camille L. Poisson
Archon Books
Connecticut, 1994

Directing for the Theatre
W. David Sievers
Wm. C. Brown, Co.
Iowa, 1965

The Director's Vision: Play Direction
from Analysis to Production
Louis E. Catron
Mayfield Publishing Co.
California, 1989

INTERNET RESOURCES

http://www.folger.edu
The Folger Shakespeare Library's
website has lesson plans, primary
sources, study guides, images,
workshops, programs for teachers
and students, and much more. The
definitive Shakespeare website for
educators, historians and all lovers
of the Bard.

http://www.shakespeare.mit.edu.
The Complete Works of
William Shakespeare.
All complete scripts for *The
30-Minute Shakespeare* series were
originally downloaded from this
site before editing. Links to other internet
resources.

http://www.LoMonico.com/
Shakespeare-and-Media.htm
http://shakespeare-and-media
.wikispaces.com
Michael LoMonico is Senior
Consultant on National Education
for the Folger Shakespeare Library.
His *Seminar Shakespeare 2.0* offers a
wealth of information on how to use
exciting new approaches and online
resources for teaching Shakespeare.

http://www.freesound.org.
A collaborative database of sounds
and sound effects.

http://www.wordle.net.
A program for creating "word clouds"
from the text that you provide. The
clouds give greater prominence to
words that appear more frequently in
the source text.

http://www.opensourceshakespeare
.org.
This site has good searching capacity.

http://shakespeare.palomar.edu/
default.htm
Excellent links and searches

http://shakespeare.com/
Write like Shakespeare,
Poetry Machine, tag cloud

http://www.shakespeare-online.com/

http://www.bardweb.net/

http://www.rhymezone.com/
shakespeare/
Good searchable word and phrase
finder.
Or by lines:
http://www.rhymezone.com/
shakespeare/toplines/

http://shakespeare.mcgill.ca/
Shakespeare and Performance
research team

http://www.enotes.com/william-
shakespeare

Needless to say, the internet goes on and on with valuable Shakespeare resources.
The ones listed here are excellent starting points and will set you on your way in the
great adventure that is Shakespeare.

NICK NEWLIN has been performing the comedy and variety act *Nicolo Whimsey* for international audiences for 27 years. Since 1996, he has conducted an annual play directing residency affiliated with the Folger Shakespeare Library in Washington, D.C. Newlin received a BA with Honors from Harvard University in 1982 and an MA in Theater with an emphasis in Play Directing from the University of Maryland in 1996.

THE 30-MINUTE SHAKESPEARE

AS YOU LIKE IT
978-1-935550-06-8

THE COMEDY OF ERRORS
978-1-935550-08-2

HAMLET
978-1-935550-24-2

HENRY IV, PART 1
978-1-935550-11-2

HENRY V
978-1-935550-38-9

JULIUS CAESAR
978-1-935550-29-7

KING LEAR
978-1-935550-09-9

LOVE'S LABOR'S LOST
978-1-935550-07-5

MACBETH
978-1-935550-02-0

A MIDSUMMER NIGHT'S DREAM
978-1-935550-00-6

THE MERCHANT OF VENICE
978-1-935550-32-7

THE MERRY WIVES OF WINDSOR
978-1-935550-05-1

MUCH ADO ABOUT NOTHING
978-1-935550-03-7

OTHELLO
978-1-935550-10-5

RICHARD III
978-1-935550-39-6

ROMEO AND JULIET
978-1-935550-01-3

THE TAMING OF THE SHREW
978-1-935550-33-4

THE TEMPEST
978-1-935550-28-0

TWELFTH NIGHT
978-1-935550-04-4

THE TWO GENTLEMEN OF VERONA
978-1-935550-25-9

THE 30-MINUTE SHAKESPEARE ANTHOLOGY
978-1-935550-33-4

All plays $9.95, available in print and eBook editions in bookstores everywhere

"A truly fun, emotional, and sometimes magical first experience . . . guided by a sagacious, knowledgeable, and intuitive educator." —Library Journal

PHOTOCOPYING AND PERFORMANCE RIGHTS

There is no royalty for performing any series of *The 30-Minute Shakespeare* in a classroom or on a stage. The publisher hereby grants unlimited photocopy permission for one series of performances to all acting groups that have purchased the play. If a group stages a performance, please post a comment and/or photo to our Facebook page; we'd love to hear about it!